Practical
Cookies

p^3

This is a P³ Book
This edition published in 2004

P³
Queen Street House
4 Queen Street
Bath BA1 1HE, UK

ISBN: 1-40542-307-2

Manufactured in China

NOTE

Cup measurements in this book are for American cups.
This book also uses imperial and metric measurements. Follow the same units
of measurement throughout; do not mix imperial and metric.
All spoon measurements are level: teaspoons are assumed to be 5 ml, and
tablespoons are assumed to be 15 ml. Unless otherwise stated,
milk is assumed to be whole milk, eggs and individual vegetables such as potatoes
are medium, and pepper is freshly ground black pepper.

The nutritional information provided for each recipe is per serving or per person.
Optional ingredients, variations, or serving suggestions have
not been included in the calculations. The times given for each recipe are an approximate
guide only because the preparation times may differ according to the techniques used by
different people and the cooking times may vary as a result of the type of oven used.

Recipes using raw or very lightly cooked eggs should be
avoided by infants, the elderly, pregnant women, convalescents,
and anyone suffering from an illness.

Contents

Introduction

What better way to spice up a coffee break than by enjoying your own freshly baked cookies? Home-baked cookies conjure up evocative images of bygone days when time appeared to stand still and people had leisure to pursue a simpler way of life. However, no one needs to miss out on this pleasurable pastime: making cookies is the easiest of all baking tasks and can easily fit into the busiest of modern lifestyles. Preparing cookies is also a great way to relieve stress: as you perform the therapeutic actions of kneading, rolling, shaping, and baking, you will feel the stress and tension literally disappear while you work. So there has never been a better time to roll up your sleeves, switch on the oven, and get baking.

Types of cookies

There are six basic types of cookie: each type is determined either by the way the dough is shaped or the way the dough is treated. Rolled cookies are the traditional type, which are made from a dough that is  rolled out. (If you find it difficult to roll out the dough thinly enough, try rolling it out between sheets of nonstick baking parchment.) These cookies are especially popular with children because the rolled-out dough can be pressed out with cookie cutters to form many fun and fancy shapes and then decorated with colored frostings after baking.

Drop cookies: these are made from a soft dough and spooned or gently pushed directly onto the cookie sheet. It is always advisable to leave a reasonable amount of space between the cookies to allow room for expansion.

Shaped cookies: these are made from a soft dough, then quickly shaped or molded into a small ball, placed on a cookie sheet, and gently flattened with the palm of the hand. If the dough sticks, do not add more flour but lightly dampen your hands.

Piped cookies: these are made from a soft dough that is piped out onto a cookie sheet. They normally have a crisp, melt-in-the-mouth texture. They are ideal to bake when large quantities are required. Often part or all of these cookies are dipped in chocolate.

Refrigerator cookies: these are an ideal standby because the dough can be made in advance and then wrapped and stored in the refrigerator for up to 1 week. When freshly baked cookies are required, simply cut off the required amount of dough and then bake it.

Bars or slices: these are formed by spreading the soft dough into a shallow, oblong pan, then they are sometimes covered with a filling or topping, and baked. After cooling slightly, they are cut into bars, slices, squares, or triangles. As with all cookies, it is always advisable to let the baked cookies cool slightly before transferring to a wire cooling rack. When cold, store them in an airtight container.

Perfect baking

When making a batch of cookies, it is important that they are all rolled or shaped to the same size and thickness so that they cook to the same level of crispness and brown evenly.

Although some ovens do not need preheating, it is important that the oven is at the correct temperature before the cookies are placed in the oven. Allow time for preheating: some ovens can take up to 15 minutes to

reach the correct temperature. Do remember that fan-assisted ovens can cook at temperatures higher than conventional ovens, so refer to the manufacturer's handbook. An oven thermometer is very useful if you are in any doubt as to the performance of your oven. Also, when baking in some ovens, it is best if the cookie sheets are placed in the middle of the oven. Do make sure that there is space around the cookie sheets for the air to circulate. This is especially important with fan-assisted ovens.

Before beginning to bake, read the recipe through beforehand to ensure that you have got all the correct ingredients and that you have allowed time for things like chilling the dough, where necessary. Collect and weigh out all the ingredients before baking and prepare your cookie sheet or pan in advance.

All cookie dough can be made by hand or in an electric mixer or food processor. If using a machine, take care not to overmix, otherwise the mixture could end up oily and difficult to work. When rolling out, use the minimum of flour for dusting, otherwise the balance of ingredients will be changed and the finished result will not be as good as it could be.

Flat, heavy cookie sheets are the best ones to use for cookies. Many doughs will be oily enough to ensure that the cookie sheets will not need greasing. However, if you find greasing is necessary, lightly oil the cookie sheet with sunflower oil, which will ensure that the cookies do not stick. Also, unlike butter or margarine, sunflower oil will not burn. Alternatively, if you prefer, you can line the cookie sheets with nonstick baking parchment or special nonstick cookie sheet liners—these cookie sheet liners are available from cookware stores and are designed specifically for baking.

Leave plenty of room for expansion during baking: ideally you should place the uncooked pieces of dough at least 2 inches/5 cm apart. If you are in doubt as to how much the dough will spread, bake one or two pieces first before baking the remaining dough.

If you are using more than one cookie sheet at a time, place the oven racks so that the oven is divided into thirds. If you find the cookies are not browning as required, move them up to the top of the oven for the last 5 minutes of the cooking time. Check the cookies a few minutes before the end of the cooking time to ensure that you do not overcook them.

Cookies that contain honey or syrup, such as florentines or brandy snaps, need a few minutes to cool on the cookie sheet before removing and placing on a wire cooling rack. However, if they are left too long, return the cookie sheet to the hot oven for a couple of minutes to soften. Otherwise, let the cookies cool slightly, remove with a wide, flexible spatula, pressing it down on the cookie sheet so as to get the spatula underneath the cookie, then transfer to wire cooling racks. If reusing the cookie sheet to bake another batch, avoid placing the uncooked dough directly onto a hot cookie sheet. Cool the cookie sheet by running cold water on the back of it, then regrease if necessary.

Storing cookies

Once cold, most freshly baked cookies should be stored in an airtight container or cookie jar. A slice of apple in the container will keep cookies moist if they are meant to be. However, store different flavors separately, and you should keep sticky or fragile cookies stored between sheets of waxed paper or baking parchment. Cookies can also be crisped quickly in a preheated oven for a few minutes, if desired.

To save time, cookie dough can usually be made ahead of time, then stored well wrapped in the refrigerator or freezer and baked as required.

KEY		
	Simplicity level 1–3 (1 easiest, 3 slightly harder)	
	Preparation time	
	Cooking time	

White Chocolate Cookies

These chunky cookies reveal a secret as you bite into them and discover the white chocolate chips scattered through them.

NUTRITIONAL INFORMATION

Calories 130	Sugars 8g	
Protein 2g	Fat 8g	
Carbohydrate ...15g	Saturates 4g	

🍰 🍰

🍯 20 mins   🕙 9–12 mins

MAKES 24

I N G R E D I E N T S

generous ½ cup butter, softened, plus extra for greasing

⅔ cup soft brown sugar

1 egg, beaten

scant 1½ cups self-rising flour

pinch of salt

4½ oz/125 g white chocolate, coarsely chopped

1¾ oz/50 g brazil nuts, chopped

1 Lightly grease several cookie sheets with a little butter.

2 In a large mixing bowl, cream together the remaining butter and the sugar, until light and fluffy.

3 Gradually add the beaten egg to the creamed mixture, beating well after each addition.

4 Sift the flour and salt into the creamed mixture and blend well.

5 Stir in the white chocolate chunks and the chopped brazil nuts.

6 Place heaped teaspoonfuls of the mixture onto the cookie sheets. Put no more than 6 on each cookie sheet to leave room for expansion during cooking.

7 Bake the cookies in a preheated oven, 375°F/190°C, for 10–12 minutes, or until just golden brown.

8 Transfer the cookies to wire racks and leave until completely cold.

VARIATION
Use semisweet or milk chocolate instead of white chocolate.

Rock Drops

These rock drops are more substantial than crisp cookies. To enjoy them at their best, serve them as soon as they have been baked.

NUTRITIONAL INFORMATION

Calories 270   Sugars 21g
Protein . . . . .4g   Fat 11g
Carbohydrate . . .41g   Saturates 7g

 15 mins   20 mins

MAKES 8

INGREDIENTS

scant ½ cup butter, cut into small pieces, plus extra for greasing

scant 1½ cups all-purpose flour

2 tsp baking powder

5 tbsp raw brown sugar

3½ oz/100 g golden raisins

1 oz/25 g candied cherries, finely chopped

1 egg, beaten

2 tbsp milk

1 Lightly grease a cookie sheet, large enough for 8 large rock drops, with a little butter.

2 Sift the flour and baking powder into a mixing bowl. Rub in the remaining butter with your fingertips, until the mixture resembles fine bread crumbs.

3 Stir in the raw brown sugar, golden raisins, and chopped candied cherries, mixing well.

4 Add the beaten egg and the milk to the mixture and mix to form a soft dough.

5 Spoon 8 mounds of the mixture onto the prepared cookie sheet, spacing them well apart because they will spread while they are cooking

6 Bake in a preheated oven, 400°F/200°C, for about 15–20 minutes, until firm to the touch

7 Remove the rock drops from the oven. Either serve piping hot from the oven, or transfer to a wire rack and let cool before serving.

COOK'S TIP

For convenience, prepare the dry ingredients in advance and stir in the liquid just before cooking.

Cheese Sablés

These crisp savory cookies combine a rich buttery flavor with the strong taste of a quality sharp hard cheese.

NUTRITIONAL INFORMATION		
Calories 67	Sugars 0g	
Protein 2g	Fat 5g	
Carbohydrate 3g	Saturates 3g	

 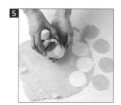 

 20 mins, plus
30 mins chilling

 20 mins

MAKES 35

INGREDIENTS

scant ¾ cup butter, cut into small pieces, plus extra for greasing

generous 1 cup all-purpose flour

1½ cups grated sharp cheese

1 egg yolk

sesame seeds, for sprinkling

1 Lightly grease several cookie sheets with a little butter.

2 Mix the flour and cheese together in a mixing bowl.

3 Add the remaining butter to the cheese and flour mixture and mix together with your fingertips.

4 Stir in the egg yolk and mix to form a dough. Wrap the dough and chill in the refrigerator for about 30 minutes.

5 On a lightly floured counter, roll out the cheese dough thinly. Cut out 2½-inch/6-cm circles.

6 Put the circles on the cookie sheets and sprinkle with the sesame seeds.

7 Bake in a preheated oven, 400°F/200°C, for 20 minutes, until the sablés are lightly golden.

8 Carefully transfer the cheese sablés to a wire rack and then let cool slightly before serving.

COOK'S TIP

Cut out any shape you like for these savory cookies. Children will like them cut into animals or other fun shapes.

Chocolate Biscotti

Italian-style dry biscuits are traditional accompaniments to black coffee after dinner, but people find themselves nibbling them the morning after.

NUTRITIONAL INFORMATION

Calories	113	Sugars	.........9g
Protein	.........2g	Fat	...........5g
Carbohydrate	...15g	Saturates	.......1g

🗖 🗖 🗖

🍫 20 mins   🕐 40 mins

MAKES 16

I N G R E D I E N T S

butter, for greasing

1 egg

½ cup superfine sugar

1 tsp vanilla extract

scant 1 cup all-purpose flour

½ tsp baking powder

1 tsp ground cinnamon

1¾ oz/50 g dark chocolate, coarsely chopped

1¾ oz/50 g toasted flaked almonds

1¾ oz/50 g pine nuts

1 Lightly grease a large cookie sheet with a little butter.

2 Whisk the egg, sugar, and vanilla extract in a mixing bowl with an electric mixer, until thick and pale—the mixture should leave a trail when the whisk is lifted.

3 Sift the flour, baking powder, and cinnamon into a separate bowl, then sift them into the egg mixture and fold in gently. Stir in the chocolate, almonds, and pine nuts.

4 Turn onto a lightly floured counter and shape into a flat log, measuring

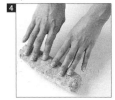

9 inches/23 cm long and ⅝ inch/1.5 cm wide. Transfer to the cookie sheet.

5 Bake in a preheated oven, 350°F/ 180°C, for 20-25 minutes, or until golden. Remove from the oven and let cool for 5 minutes, or until firm.

6 Transfer the log to a cutting board. Using a serrated bread knife, cut the

log diagonally into slices about ½ inch/ 1 cm thick and arrange them on the cookie sheet. Return to the oven for about 10-15 minutes, turning the biscotti over onto the other side halfway through the cooking time to bake evenly.

7 Let the cookies cool for about 5 minutes, then transfer to a wire rack to cool completely.

Persian Rice Crescents

These little cookies made with rice flour have a fine texture and a delicate flavor. They are excellent with strong black coffee.

NUTRITIONAL INFORMATION	
Calories 58	Sugars 2g
Protein 1g	Fat 4g
Carbohydrate 5g	Saturates 2g

30 mins, plus 1 hr resting   15 mins

MAKES 60

INGREDIENTS

1 cup unsalted butter, softened, plus extra for greasing

scant ⅔ cup confectioners' sugar, sifted

2 egg yolks

½–1 tsp ground cardamom or 1 tbsp rosewater

1¾ cups rice flour, sifted

1 egg white, lightly beaten

½ cup finely chopped pistachios or almonds

1 Lightly grease several cookie sheets with a little butter.

2 Using an electric mixer, beat the remaining butter in a large bowl, until light and creamy. Gradually add the confectioners' sugar and beat for about 2 minutes, until light and fluffy. Gradually add the egg yolks, beating well after each addition. Add the cardamom and the rice flour and mix in to a soft dough.

3 Turn the dough onto a lightly floured counter and knead lightly. Turn the mixing bowl over the dough and let rest for about 1 hour.

4 Form heaped teaspoonfuls of the dough into balls, then form into crescent shapes. Place 2 inches/5 cm apart on the prepared cookie sheets. Mark a pattern on the tops with a spoon.

5 Brush each crescent with a little beaten egg white and sprinkle with the chopped nuts.

6 Bake in a preheated oven, 350°C/ 180°F, for about 15 minutes, until the bottoms begin to color; the tops should remain very pale. Reduce the heat if the tops begin to color.

7 Cool on the cookie sheets for about 2 minutes, then transfer the cookies to wire racks to cool completely. Dust with confectioners' sugar before serving.

COOK'S TIP

Cooking-oil sprays are ideal for greasing cookie sheets lightly for baking cookies.

Lemon Bites

These lemon-flavored, melt-in-the-mouth cookies are given
a luxurious dredging with confectioners' sugar just before serving.

NUTRITIONAL INFORMATION

Calories	50	Sugars	.........3g
Protein	.........1g	Fat	..........2g
Carbohydrate	....8g	Saturates	.......1g

25 mins   20 mins

MAKES 50

INGREDIENTS

scant ½ cup butter, softened, plus extra
  for greasing

⅔ cup superfine sugar

grated rind of 1 lemon

1 egg, beaten

4 tbsp lemon juice

2½ cups all-purpose flour

1 tsp baking powder

1 tbsp milk

confectioners' sugar, for dredging

 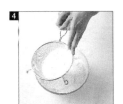 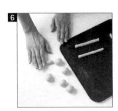

1 Lightly grease several cookie sheets
with a little butter.

2 In a mixing bowl, cream together the
remaining butter, superfine sugar, and
lemon rind, until pale and fluffy.

3 Add the beaten egg and lemon juice,
a little at a time, beating well after
each addition.

4 Sift the flour and baking powder into
the creamed mixture and blend
together. Add the milk, mixing it in to
form a soft dough.

5 Turn the dough out onto a lightly
floured counter and divide into about
50 equal-size pieces.

6 Roll each piece into a sausage shape
with your hands and bend in the
middle to make an "S" shape.

7 Place on the prepared cookie sheets
and bake in a preheated oven 325°F/
160°C, for 15–20 minutes. Carefully transfer
to a wire rack and set aside to cool
completely. Dredge with confectioners'
sugar and serve.

VARIATION
Form the dough into other
shapes—letters of the alphabet
or geometric shapes—or just
make it into round cookies.

Vanilla Hearts

This is a classic shortbread cookie, cut into appealing heart shapes and light enough to melt into your taste buds.

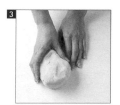

NUTRITIONAL INFORMATION

Calories	150	Sugars	.........9g
Protein	.........1g	Fat	..........8g
Carbohydrate	...20g	Saturates	.......5g

 15 mins   20 mins

MAKES 12

I N G R E D I E N T S

scant ¾ cup butter, cut into small pieces, plus extra for greasing

generous 1½ cups all-purpose flour

⅔ cup superfine sugar, plus extra for dusting

1 tsp vanilla extract

1 Lightly grease a cookie sheet with a little butter.

2 Sift the flour into a large mixing bowl and rub in the remaining butter with your fingertips, until the mixture resembles fine bread crumbs.

3 Stir in the superfine sugar and vanilla extract and mix into a firm dough with your hands.

COOK'S TIP

Place a fresh vanilla bean in your superfine sugar and keep it in a storage jar for several weeks to give the sugar a delicious vanilla flavor.

4 On a lightly floured counter, roll out the vanilla dough to a thickness of 1 inch/2.5 cm. Stamp out 12 hearts using a heart-shaped cookie cutter measuring about 2 inches/5 cm across and 1 inch/2.5 cm deep.

5 Arrange the heart-shaped cookies on the prepared cookie sheet. Bake in a preheated oven, 350°F/180°C, for about 15-20 minutes, until the hearts have baked to a light golden color.

6 Transfer the vanilla hearts to a wire rack and leave them until they have cooled completely. When you are ready to serve them, transfer them to a serving plate and dust with a little superfine sugar.

Oat & Raisin Cookies

These oaty, fruity cookies couldn't be easier to make and are delicious served with a creamy rum and raisin ice cream.

NUTRITIONAL INFORMATION	
Calories 227	Sugars 22g
Protein 4g	Fat 7g
Carbohydrate ...39g	Saturates 3g

🍦 50 mins   🕐 15 mins

SERVES 4

I N G R E D I E N T S

4 tbsp butter, plus extra for greasing

⅔ cup superfine sugar

1 egg, beaten

½ cup all-purpose flour

½ tsp salt

½ tsp baking powder

1¾ cups rolled oats

scant 1 cup raisins

2 tbsp sesame seeds

1 Lightly grease 2 cookie sheets with a little butter.

2 In a large mixing bowl, cream together the remaining butter and the sugar, until light and fluffy.

3 Gradually add the beaten egg, beating well after each addition, until thoroughly combined.

4 Sift the flour, salt, and baking powder into the creamed mixture. Mix gently to combine. Add the rolled oats, raisins, and sesame seeds and mix together, until thoroughly combined.

5 Place spoonfuls of the mixture on the prepared cookie sheets, spaced well apart to leave room for expansion during cooking, and flatten them slightly with the back of a spoon.

6 Bake the cookies in a preheated oven, 350°F/180°C, for 15 minutes.

7 Let the cookies cool slightly on the cookie sheets, then carefully transfer them to a wire rack and set aside to cool completely before serving.

COOK'S TIP

To enjoy these cookies at their best, store them in an airtight container.

Lemon Chocolate Pinwheels

Make these stunning cookies for a special occasion. They look impressive and their intriguing taste will be a talking point.

NUTRITIONAL INFORMATION

Calories 97	Sugars 8g	
Protein 1g	Fat 4g	
Carbohydrate ...15g	Saturates 3g	

 30 mins, plus 30 mins chilling   🕐 12 mins

MAKES 40

I N G R E D I E N T S

¾ cup butter, softened, plus extra for greasing

2½ cups all-purpose flour, plus extra for dusting

generous 1½ cups superfine sugar

1 egg, beaten

1 oz/25 g dark chocolate, melted and cooled slightly

grated rind of 1 lemon

1 Lightly grease several cookie sheets and dust them with flour.

2 In a large mixing bowl, cream together the remaining butter and the sugar, until light and fluffy.

3 Gradually add the beaten egg to the creamed mixture, beating thoroughly.

4 Sift the remaining flour into the creamed mixture and mix thoroughly, until a soft dough forms.

5 Transfer half of the dough to another bowl and then beat in the cooled melted chocolate.

6 Stir the grated lemon rind into the other half of the plain dough.

7 On a lightly floured counter, roll out the 2 pieces of dough to form rectangles of the same size.

8 Lay the lemon dough on top of the chocolate dough. Roll up the dough tightly into a sausage shape, using a sheet of baking parchment to guide you. Leave the dough to chill in the refrigerator, until firm enough to slice.

9 Cut the roll into about 40 slices, place them on the prepared cookie sheets and bake in a preheated oven, 375°F/ 190°C, for 10–12 minutes, or until lightly golden. Transfer the pinwheels to a wire rack and let cool completely before serving.

 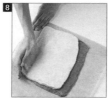 

COOK'S TIP

To make rolling out easier, place each piece of dough between 2 sheets of baking parchment.

Savory Curried Cookies

For these cookies, you will need to experiment with different strengths of curry powder, until you find the one that suits your taste.

NUTRITIONAL INFORMATION

Calories	48	Sugars	.........0g
Protein	.........2g	Fat	..........4g
Carbohydrate	....2g	Saturates	.......2g

 20 mins   🕐 15 mins

MAKES 40

I N G R E D I E N T S

scant ½ cup butter, diced and softened, plus extra for greasing

¾ cup all-purpose flour, plus extra for dusting

1 tsp salt

2 tsp curry powder

1 cup grated Cheshire cheese

1 cup freshly grated Parmesan cheese

1 Lightly grease several cookie sheets with a little butter.

2 Sift the all-purpose flour and salt into a mixing bowl.

3 Stir in the curry powder and the grated Cheshire and Parmesan cheeses. Rub in the remaining softened butter with your fingertips, until the mixture comes together to form a soft dough.

4 On a lightly floured counter, roll out the dough thinly into a rectangle.

5 Using a 2-inch/5-cm cookie cutter, cut out 40 round cookies.

6 Arrange the cookies on the prepared cookie sheets.

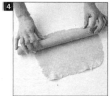

7 Bake the cookies in a preheated oven, 350°F/180°C, for 10–15 minutes, until the cookies have turned a deep golden brown.

8 Let the cookies cool slightly on the cookie sheets. Then transfer them carefully to a wire rack and leave them until they are completely cold and crisp before serving them.

COOK'S TIP

These cookies can be stored for several days in an airtight tin or a plastic container.

Gingernuts

A hint of orange gives these old favorites an unusual touch and a memorable flavor, making them worthy of a special snacktime treat.

NUTRITIONAL INFORMATION

Calories	106	Sugars	9g
Protein	1g	Fat	4g
Carbohydrate	18g	Saturates	2g

🜃 20 mins   🕐 20 mins

MAKES 30

INGREDIENTS

generous ½ cup butter, plus extra for greasing

2½ cups self-rising flour

pinch of salt

1 cup superfine sugar

1 tbsp ground ginger

1 tsp baking soda

⅓ cup corn syrup

1 egg, beaten

1 tsp grated orange rind

1 Lightly grease several cookie sheets with a little butter.

2 Sift the flour, salt, sugar, ginger, and baking soda together into a large mixing bowl.

3 Melt the butter and golden syrup together in a pan over very low heat.

4 Remove the pan from the heat and let the butter and syrup mixture cool slightly, then pour it onto the dry ingredients and stir together.

5 Add the egg and orange rind and mix thoroughly to form a dough.

6 Using your hands, carefully shape the dough into 30 even-size balls.

7 Place the balls well apart on the prepared cookie sheets, then flatten them slightly with your fingers.

8 Bake in a preheated oven, 325°F/ 160°C, for 15–20 minutes, until golden. Carefully transfer the cookies to a wire rack to cool.

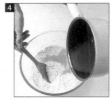

COOK'S TIP

If you prefer, use preserved or grated fresh ginger in place of ground dried ginger.

Spiced Cookies

These sweet cookies are strongly spiced, and served with fruit salad or ice cream they make an instant summer dessert.

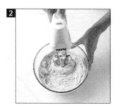

NUTRITIONAL INFORMATION

Calories 117	Sugars 8g	
Protein 1g	Fat 6g	
Carbohydrate . . .15g	Saturates 4g	

🕒 15 mins   🕐 12 mins

MAKES 12

I N G R E D I E N T S

¾ cup unsalted butter, plus extra for greasing

scant 1 cup molasses sugar

generous 1½ cups all-purpose flour

pinch of salt

½ tsp baking soda

1 tsp ground cinnamon

½ tsp ground coriander

½ tsp ground nutmeg

¼ tsp ground cloves

2 tbsp dark rum

1 Lightly grease 2 cookie sheets with a little butter.

2 Cream together the remaining butter and the sugar in a mixing bowl and whisk together, until light and fluffy.

3 Sift together the flour, salt, baking soda, cinnamon, coriander, nutmeg, and cloves and stir them gently into the creamed mixture.

4 Stir the dark rum into the creamed mixture, mixing in well.

5 Using 2 teaspoons, place small mounds of the mixture on the cookie sheets, placing them 2¾ inches/7 cm apart

to leave plenty of room for them to spread out during cooking. Flatten each one slightly with the back of a spoon.

6 Bake in a preheated oven, 350°F/ 180°C, for 10–12 minutes, until the cookies are golden.

7 Carefully transfer the cookies to wire racks to cool completely and go crisp before serving them.

COOK'S TIP

Use the back of a fork to flatten the cookies slightly before baking to give them a grooved appearance.

Caraway Cookies

The caraway seed is best known for its appearance in old-fashioned seed cake. Here, caraway seeds give these cookies a distinctive flavor.

NUTRITIONAL INFORMATION

Calories	69	Sugars	.........7g
Protein	.........1g	Fat	..........3g
Carbohydrate	....11g	Saturates	.......2g

🥘 15 mins   🕐 15 mins

MAKES 36

INGREDIENTS

scant ½ cup butter, cut into small pieces, plus extra for greasing

generous 1½ cups all-purpose flour

pinch of salt

generous 1 cup superfine sugar

1 egg, beaten

2 tbsp caraway seeds

raw brown sugar, for sprinkling

1 Lightly grease several cookie sheets with a little butter.

2 Sift the flour and salt into a mixing bowl. Rub in the remaining butter with your fingertips, until the mixture resembles fine bread crumbs. Stir in the superfine sugar.

3 Reserve 1 tablespoon of the beaten egg for brushing the cookies. Add the rest of the egg to the mixture along with the caraway seeds and bring together to form a soft dough.

4 On a lightly floured counter, roll out the cookie dough thinly and then cut out about 36 circles with a 2½-inch/6-cm cookie cutter.

5 Transfer the circles to the prepared cookie sheets, brush with the reserved egg, and sprinkle with raw brown sugar.

6 Bake in a preheated oven, 325°F/160°C, for 10-15 minutes, until lightly golden and crisp.

7 Let the cookies cool on a wire rack and store in an airtight container.

VARIATION

Caraway seeds have a delicate anise flavor, which may be an acquired taste. Poppy seeds make a good substitute.

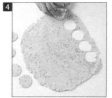

Rosemary Cookies

Aromatic herbs are an unfamiliar cookie ingredient and they turn these crisp cookies into a new experience for the taste buds.

NUTRITIONAL INFORMATION

Calories	50	Sugars	.........2g
Protein	.........1g	Fat	..........2g
Carbohydrate	....8g	Saturates	.......1g

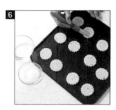

🕐 20 mins, plus 30 mins chilling   🕐 15 mins

MAKES 25

I N G R E D I E N T S

scant ¼ cup butter, softened, plus extra for greasing

4 tbsp superfine sugar

grated rind of 1 lemon

4 tbsp lemon juice

1 egg, separated

2 tsp finely chopped fresh rosemary

scant 1½ cups all-purpose flour, sifted

superfine sugar, for sprinkling (optional)

1 Lightly grease 2 cookie sheets with a little butter.

2 In a large mixing bowl, cream together the remaining butter and the sugar, until the mixture is pale and fluffy.

3 Add the lemon rind and juice, then the egg yolk and beat until the mixture is thoroughly blended. Stir in the chopped fresh rosemary.

4 Add the sifted flour, mixing well, until a soft dough is formed. Wrap and let chill for 30 minutes.

5 On a lightly floured counter, roll out the dough thinly and then stamp out 25 circles with a 2½-inch/6-cm cookie cutter. Arrange the dough circles on the prepared cookie sheets.

6 In a small bowl, lightly whisk the egg white with a fork. Gently brush the egg white over the surface of each cookie to glaze, then sprinkle over a little superfine sugar, if desired.

7 Bake the cookies in a preheated oven 350°F/180°C, for about 15 minutes until golden.

8 Transfer the cookies to a wire rack and let cool before serving.

COOK'S TIP
Store the cookies in an airtight container and keep for up to 1 week.

Peanut Butter Cookies

Every kid's favorite food is baked into these crunchy cookies to make them a certain hit with children of all ages.

NUTRITIONAL INFORMATION	
Calories 186	Sugars 13g
Protein 4g	Fat 11g
Carbohydrate ...19g	Saturates 5g

🍪 20 mins, plus 30 mins chilling ⏱ 15 mins

MAKES 20

INGREDIENTS

generous ½ cup butter, softened, plus extra for greasing

¾ cup crunchy peanut butter

generous 1 cup granulated sugar

1 egg, lightly beaten

generous 1 cup all-purpose flour

½ tsp baking powder

pinch of salt

½ cup natural unsalted peanuts, chopped

1 Lightly grease 2 cookie sheets with a little butter.

2 In a bowl, beat together the remaining butter and the peanut butter.

3 Gradually add the granulated sugar and beat well.

4 Add the beaten egg, a little at a time, beating well after each addition, until it is thoroughly combined.

5 Sift the flour, baking powder, and salt into the peanut butter mixture.

6 Add the chopped peanuts and bring all of the ingredients together to form a soft dough. Wrap the dough in plastic wrap and let chill in the refrigerator for about 30 minutes.

7 Form the dough into 20 balls and place them on the prepared cookie sheets about 2 inches/5 cm apart to leave room for spreading. Flatten them slightly with the ends of your fingers.

8 Bake in a preheated oven, 375°F/ 190°C, for 15 minutes, until golden brown. Transfer the biscuits to a wire rack and let cool.

COOK'S TIP
For a crunchy bite and sparkling appearance, sprinkle the cookies with raw brown sugar before baking.

Citrus Crescents

For a sweet treat, try these attractive crescent-shaped cookies, which have a reviving citrus tang in every bite.

NUTRITIONAL INFORMATION

Calories 72   Sugars 3g
Protein ....1g   Fat 4g
Carbohydrate ...10g   Saturates 2g

20 mins   15 mins

MAKES 25

INGREDIENTS

scant ½ cup butter, softened, plus extra for greasing

5 tbsp superfine sugar, plus extra for sprinkling (optional)

1 egg, separated

scant 1½ cups all-purpose flour

grated rind of 1 orange

grated rind of 1 lemon

grated rind of 1 lime

2–3 tbsp orange juice

1 Lightly grease 2 cookie sheets with a little butter.

2 In a mixing bowl, cream together the remaining butter and the sugar, until light and fluffy, then beat in the egg yolk.

3 Sift the flour into the creamed mixture and mix in, until evenly combined. Add the orange, lemon, and lime rinds to the mixture with enough of the orange juice to make a soft dough.

4 Roll out the dough on a lightly floured counter. Stamp out circles using a 3-inch/7.5-cm cookie cutter. Make crescents by cutting away a little of each circle with the cutter. Reroll the trimmings to make about 25 crescents.

5 Place the crescents on the prepared cookie sheets. Prick the surface of each crescent with a fork.

6 Lightly whisk the egg white in a small bowl and brush it over the cookies. Sprinkle with extra superfine sugar, if using.

7 Bake in a preheated oven, 400°F/ 200°C, for 12–15 minutes. Carefully transfer the cookies to a wire rack and then let cool completely and go crisp before serving.

COOK'S TIP
You can store the citrus crescents in an airtight container. Alternatively, keep them frozen for up to 1 month.

Almond Cookies

Almond trees grow in abundance all over the Mediterranean region, so the slightly sweet nut appears frequently in regional cookies.

NUTRITIONAL INFORMATION

Calories	121	Sugars	3g
Protein	2g	Fat	8g
Carbohydrate	10g	Saturates	4g

 25 mins   25 mins

MAKES 32

I N G R E D I E N T S

1 cup unblanched almonds

1 cup butter, softened

6 tbsp confectioners' sugar, plus extra
  for sifting

2 cups all-purpose flour

2 tsp vanilla extract

½ tsp almond extract

1 Line 2 cookie sheets with baking parchment. Finely chop the almonds, or process them in a small food processor, taking care not to let them turn into a paste. Set aside.

2 Put the butter in a bowl and beat with an electric mixer, until smooth. Sift in the confectioners' sugar and continue beating, until creamed and smooth.

3 Sift in the flour from above the bowl and beat it in, until blended. Add the vanilla and almond extracts and beat the mixture again to form a soft dough. Stir in the chopped almonds.

4 Using a teaspoon, shape the dough into 32 round balls about the size of walnuts. Place on the prepared cookie sheets, spacing them apart. Bake in a preheated oven, 350°F/180°C, for 20–25 minutes, until set and just starting to turn brown.

5 Let the cookies stand on the cookie sheets for 2 minutes to firm up. Sift a thick layer of confectioners' sugar over them. Transfer to a wire rack and let cool completely.

6 Lightly dust with more confectioners' sugar, just before serving. Store in an airtight container for up to one week.

VARIATION
Pecans may be used instead of almonds. Add two teaspoons of finely grated orange rind to the dough in step 3.

Chocolate Coconut Squares

These cookies consist of a chewy coconut layer resting on a crisp chocolate cookie bottom, cut into squares to serve.

NUTRITIONAL INFORMATION

Calories 400	Sugars 17g	
Protein 6g	Fat 27g	
Carbohydrate ...36g	Saturates 18g	

1¼ hrs   30 mins

MAKES 9

INGREDIENTS

⅓ cup butter or margarine, plus extra for greasing

8 oz/225 g dark chocolate graham crackers

¾ cup canned evaporated milk

1 egg, beaten

1 tsp vanilla extract

2 tbsp superfine sugar

⅓ cup self-rising flour, sifted

1⅓ cups shredded coconut

1¾ oz/50 g dark chocolate, optional

1 Grease a shallow 8-inch/20-cm square cake pan with butter and line the bottom.

2 Crush the crackers in a plastic bag with a rolling pin or process them in a food processor.

3 Melt the remaining butter in a pan and stir in the crushed crackers.

4 Press the mixture into the bottom of the cake pan.

5 Beat together the evaporated milk, egg, vanilla, and sugar, until smooth. Stir in the flour and shredded coconut. Pour over the cracker layer and use a spatula to level the top.

6 Bake in a preheated oven, 375°F/190°C, for 30 minutes, or until the coconut topping has become firm and just golden.

7 Let cool in the cake pan for 5 minutes, then cut into squares. Let cool completely in the pan.

8 Carefully remove the squares from the pan and place them on a cutting board. Melt the dark chocolate, if using, and drizzle it over the squares. Let the chocolate set before serving.

COOK'S TIP

Store the squares in an airtight container for up to 4 days. They can be frozen, undecorated, for up to 2 months. Thaw at room temperature.

Dutch Macaroons

These unusual cookie treats are delicious served with coffee. They also make an ideal dessert cookie to serve with ice cream.

NUTRITIONAL INFORMATION

Calories 158	Sugars 19g	
Protein 3g	Fat 8g	
Carbohydrate ...20g	Saturates 2g	

🍪 🍪 🍪

🍪 40 mins   🕐 15–20 mins

MAKES 20

INGREDIENTS

rice paper

2 egg whites

1 cup superfine sugar

1⅔ cups ground almonds

8 oz/225 g dark chocolate

1 Cover 2 cookie sheets with rice paper. Whisk the egg whites in a large mixing bowl until stiff, then fold in the sugar and ground almonds.

2 Place the mixture in a large pastry bag fitted with a ½-inch/1-cm plain tip. Pipe fingers, about 3 inches/ 7.5 cm long, leaving space for the mixture to spread during cooking.

3 Bake in a preheated oven, 350°F/ 180°C, for 15–20 minutes, until

golden. Transfer to a wire rack and let cool. Remove the excess rice paper from around the edges.

4 Melt the chocolate and dip the bottom of each cookie into the chocolate. Place the macaroons on a sheet of baking parchment and let set.

5 Drizzle any remaining chocolate over the top of the cookies (you may need to reheat the chocolate in order to do this). Let it set before serving.

COOK'S TIP

Rice paper is edible so you can break off just the excess from around the edges of the cookies, or remove it completely before dipping in the chocolate, if you prefer.

Chocolate & Coconut Cookies

These delicious, melt-in-the-mouth cookies are finished off with a simple gooey frosting and a generous sprinkling of coconut.

NUTRITIONAL INFORMATION

Calories 117	Sugars 7g	
Protein 1g	Fat 8g	
Carbohydrate . . .12g	Saturates 3g	

40 mins   12–15 mins

MAKES 24

INGREDIENTS

½ cup soft margarine, plus extra for greasing

1 tsp vanilla extract

½ cup confectioners' sugar, sifted

1 cup all-purpose flour

2 tbsp unsweetened cocoa

⅔ cup shredded coconut

2 tbsp butter

3½ oz/100 g white marshmallows

⅓ cup shredded coconut

a little white chocolate, grated

1 Lightly grease a cookie sheet with margarine. Beat the remaining margarine with the vanilla and sugar in a mixing bowl, until fluffy. Sift together the flour and cocoa and beat it into the mixture with the coconut.

2 Roll rounded teaspoons of the mixture into balls; place on the cookie sheet, leaving room for expansion during cooking.

3 Flatten the balls slightly and bake in a preheated oven, 350°F/180°C, for 12–15 minutes, until just firm.

4 Let cool on the cookie sheet for a few minutes before transferring to a wire rack to cool completely.

5 Place the butter and marshmallows in a small pan and heat gently, stirring, until melted. Spread a little of the frosting mixture over each cookie and dip in the coconut. Let them set. Decorate with grated white chocolate before serving.

Viennese Chocolate Fingers

These cookies have a fabulously light, melting texture. You can leave them plain, but for real indulgence dip them in chocolate to decorate.

NUTRITIONAL INFORMATION

Calories	170	Sugars	........12g
Protein	.........1g	Fat	..........9g
Carbohydrate	...22g	Saturates	......6g

🍮 1 hr   🕐 12–15 mins

MAKES 18

I N G R E D I E N T S

½ cup unsalted butter, plus extra for greasing

6 tbsp confectioners' sugar

1½ cups self-rising flour, sifted

3 tbsp cornstarch

7 oz/200 g dark chocolate

1 Lightly grease 2 cookie sheets with butter. Beat the remaining butter and the sugar in a mixing bowl, until light and fluffy. Gradually beat in the flour and the cornstarch.

2 Melt 2¾ oz/75 g of the dark chocolate and beat it into the cookie dough.

3 Place the mixture in a pastry bag fitted with a large star tip and pipe fingers 2 inches/5 cm long on the cookie sheets, spaced apart to leave room for spreading.

COOK'S TIP

If the cookie dough is too thick to pipe, beat in a little milk to thin it out.

4 Bake in a preheated oven, 375°F/ 190°C, for 12–15 minutes. Let cool slightly on the cookie sheets, then use a spatula to transfer to a wire rack. Let the cookies cool completely.

5 Melt the remaining chocolate and dip one end of each cookie into the chocolate, letting the excess drip back into the bowl.

6 Place the cookies on a sheet of baking parchment and let the chocolate set before serving.

Chocolate Hazelnut Palmiers

These delicious chocolate and hazelnut cookes are very simple to make, yet so effective. For very young children, leave out the chopped nuts.

NUTRITIONAL INFORMATION

Calories	113	Sugars	.........6g
Protein	.........2g	Fat	..........7g
Carbohydrate	....11g	Saturates	......1g

 5 mins

 10–15 mins

MAKES 26

INGREDIENTS

TOPPING

1 tbsp butter, for greasing

13 oz/375 g ready-made puff pie dough

8 tbsp chocolate hazelnut spread

½ cup chopped toasted hazelnuts

2 tbsp superfine sugar

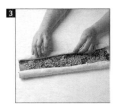
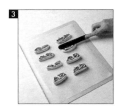

1 Lightly grease a cookie sheet with butter. On a lightly floured counter, roll out the puff pie dough to a rectangle about 15 x 9 inches/38 x 23 cm in size.

2 Using a spatula, spread the chocolate hazelnut spread over the pie dough and then scatter the chopped hazelnuts over the top.

3 Roll up one long side of the pie dough to the center, then roll up the other side so that they meet in the middle. Where the pieces meet, dampen the edges with a little water to join them. Using a sharp knife, cut into thin slices. Place each slice onto the prepared cookie sheet and flatten slightly with the spatula. Sprinkle the slices with the superfine sugar.

4 Bake in a preheated oven, 425°F/ 220°C, for about 10–15 minutes, until golden. Transfer to a wire rack to cool.

VARIATION

For an extra chocolate flavor, dip the palmiers in melted dark chocolate to cover half of each cookie.

Chocolate Caramel Squares

It is difficult to resist these marvelously rich cookies, which consist of a crunchy oat layer, a creamy caramel filling, and a chocolate top.

NUTRITIONAL INFORMATION	
Calories 193	Sugars 18g
Protein 3g	Fat 9g
Carbohydrate ...26g	Saturates 3g

 40 mins   🕐 25 mins

MAKES 16

INGREDIENTS

generous ⅓ cup soft margarine

⅓ cup light brown sugar

generous 1 cup all-purpose flour

½ cup rolled oats

CARAMEL FILLING

2 tbsp butter

2 tbsp light brown sugar

generous ¾ cup condensed milk

TOPPING

3½ oz/100 g dark chocolate

1 oz/25 g white chocolate, optional

1 Beat together the margarine and brown sugar in a bowl, until light and fluffy. Beat in the flour and the rolled oats. Use your fingertips to bring the mixture together, if necessary.

COOK'S TIP

If desired, you can line the pan with baking parchment so that the oat layer can be lifted out before cutting into pieces.

2 Press the oat mixture into the bottom of a shallow 8-inch/20-cm square cake pan.

3 Bake in a preheated oven, 350°F/180°C, for 25 minutes, or until just golden and firm. Cool in the pan.

4 Place the ingredients for the caramel filling in a pan and heat gently, stirring, until the sugar has dissolved and the ingredients combine. Bring slowly to a boil over very low heat, then boil very

gently for 3–4 minutes, stirring constantly, until thickened.

5 Pour the caramel filling over the oat layer in the pan and let set.

6 Melt the dark chocolate and spread it over the caramel. If using the white chocolate, melt it and pipe lines of white chocolate over the dark chocolate. Using a toothpick or skewer, feather the white chocolate into the dark chocolate. Let set. Cut into squares to serve.